Contents

Introduction

All countries and cultures celebrate special days throughout the year.

This man is reading from the Sikh holy book in celebration of the birthday of **Guru Nanek Dev**.

A World of Festivals

Special Days
and Holidays

Jean Coppendale

Chrysalis Children's Books

First published in the UK in 2003 by
Chrysalis Children's Books
An imprint of Chrysalis Books Group Plc
The Chrysalis Building, Bramley Road, London W10 6SP

Paperback edition first published in 2005

ISBN 1 84138 845 9 (hb)
ISBN 1 84458 489 5 (pb)

British Library Cataloguing in Publication Data for this book is available from the British Library.

Editorial Manager: Joyce Bentley
Assistant Editor: Clare Chambers
Produced by Tall Tree Ltd
Editor: Jon Richards
Consultant: Stephanie Batley
Picture Researcher: Dan Brooks
Artwork: Piers Harper

Printed in China

10 9 8 7 6 5 4 3 2 1

PICTURE CREDITS
All reasonable efforts have been made to trace the relevant copyright holders of the images contained within this book. If we were unable to reach you, please contact Chrysalis Books.

B = bottom; C = centre; L = left; R = right; T = top.
Corbis – 9, 17, 23. **Christine Osborne Pictures** – 16. **Eye Ubiquitous** – back cover, 1, 4, 5, 6, 10, 14, 22, 24, 25, 26, 27. **Katz Pictures** – 11. **Paul Nightingale** – front cover BR, 7, 12, 15. **Spectrum Colour Library** – front cover, 8, 13, 18, 19, 20, 21.

Special days and holidays can be times when people simply get together to have fun and to sing and dance.

This street carnival is to celebrate the Battle of the Flowers on the British island of Jersey.

Sometimes the days are special because a well-known person was born on that day or it is a day when an important person is remembered.

Happy New Year

Different cultures around the world start the year at different times. But they all start it with a party.

One feature of Songkran is the water festival when people throw water for fun.

Songkran

This is the New Year festival in Thailand. Firecrackers are set off to drive away bad luck, and people go to special services at their local temples.

Honey and apples are eaten at Rosh Hashanah.

Rosh Hashanah

Rosh Hashanah is the Jewish New Year. People go to the **synagogue** to ask God to forgive their sins. After this service, families go home for a special meal.

FESTIVAL DIARY

Rosh Hashanah
Jewish
September or October

Songkran
Thailand
April

7

Dragon Dances

New Year's festivals are some of the oldest of all celebrations in the world.

A beautiful dragon is carried through the streets for the Chinese New Year.

Chinese New Year

These celebrations are very colourful and noisy. People say 'kung hay fat choi', wishing each other health and wealth.

People decorate the streets with tree **blossoms** for Tet.

Tet

Tet, or Tet Nguyen-Dan, lasts for seven days. Bright lights and paper decorations are put up in the streets, and dragon and unicorn dances are performed.

FESTIVAL DIARY

New Year
China
21 January to
20 February

Tet
Vietnam
February

Ramadan

Ramadan is one of the most important Muslim festivals. It is celebrated by Muslims all over the world.

During Ramadan, Muslims go to the **mosque** and say special prayers, including the Taraweeh, or night prayer.

Holy book
Ramadan celebrates the time when the **Qu'ran**, the Muslim holy book, was first sent down by God to the **Prophet** Mohammed.

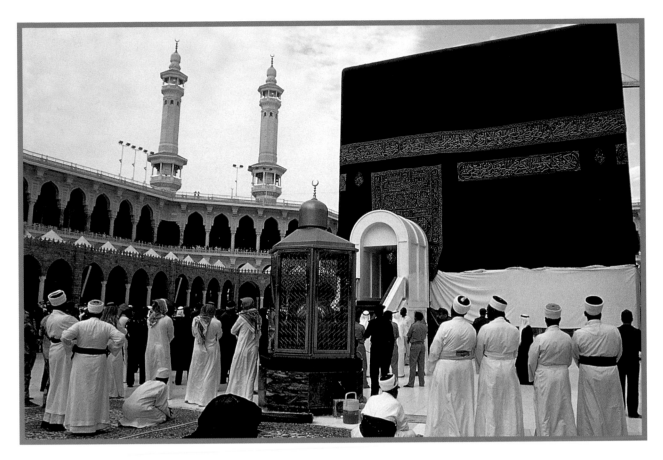

Many Muslims visit the holy city of Mecca in Saudi Arabia for Ramadan. Here they visit the sacred **shrine**, or **Ka'aba**.

Fasting

The festival lasts for about a month. During this time, Muslims do not eat anything between sunrise and sunset.

FESTIVAL DIARY

Ramadan
Muslim
November and December

National Days

Many countries have celebrations to remember important events in their history.

Many Americans fly the American flag outside their homes.

Independence

Independence Day celebrates July 4, 1776, when the American people broke away from British rule. All over the country there are **parades**, street parties, and firework displays.

Fireworks explode over the Australian city of Sydney.

Australia Day

This festival remembers the arrival of the first European settlers to Australia in 1788. Today, people also remember the rights of Australian **Aborigines**, whose land was taken by these early settlers.

FESTIVAL DIARY

Independence Day
United States
July 4

Australia Day
Australia
January 26

Saints' Days

The lives of Christian saints are celebrated by countries all over the world on special saints' days.

Saint Patrick's Day is celebrated with parades and parties, and people dress up in green and wear shamrocks.

Saint Patrick
Saint Patrick is the **patron saint** of Ireland. There are many stories about him, including how he drove all the snakes out of Ireland.

People give their loved ones cards, flowers and presents for Valentine's Day.

Saint Valentine

Many years ago, a man called Valentine was arrested for helping Christians. In jail, he fell in love with the jailer's daughter and gave her a note signed 'from your Valentine'.

FESTIVAL DIARY

Saint Patrick's Day
Ireland, United States, United Kingdom
17 March

Valentine's Day
Europe, United States
14 February

Crop Festivals

The planting and harvesting of crops has always been celebrated by people around the world.

During O-Taue, girls plant rice plants to the sound of traditional instruments.

Rice Festival

The Japanese Rice Festival is called O-Taue. Young men, called tachido, give young rice plants to girls, who are called saotome.

Families light seven candles that are black, green and red for Kwanzaa.

Kwanzaa

This seven-day festival is celebrated by African-Americans. Kwanzaa means 'first fruits' and is held to celebrate the year's **harvest** in Africa.

FESTIVAL DIARY

O-Taue
Japan
1 June

Kwanzaa
United States and the Caribbean
26 December

17

Flower Festivals

Many festivals and parades celebrate the beauty of flowers.

Cherry blossom is the national flower of Japan.

Sakura

During the spring festival of Sakura in Japan, huge crowds of people picnic under the cherry trees which are covered in blossoms.

Only flowers that are grown on Jersey can be used to cover the floats in the Battle of the Flowers.

Flower battle

The Battle of the Flowers is a competition in which floats are judged to see which is the best in the parade. The floats are judged on design, colour and size.

FESTIVAL DIARY

Sakura
Japan
Early April

Battle of the Flowers
Jersey,
Channel Islands, UK
August

19

The Palio

The Palio is a famous horse race and parade which takes place in the town of Siena, Italy.

In the Palio, each rider wears the colours of his district.

The race

The town is divided into 17 districts, and each district enters a horse and rider. During the Palio, horses and riders race around the town square.

During the victory parade, people wave huge flags and throw them high in the air.

A parade
The day after the race, the people, the jockey and the horse from the winning district parade through the streets of Siena with a marching band.

FESTIVAL DIARY

Palio
Italy
July or August

Boat Races

Many festivals around the world feature exciting boat races – although not all of them happen on the water!

Dragon boats are paddled by lots of people.

Dragon Boat Festival
Long, thin boats decorated with dragons' heads are raced to celebrate the beginning of summer.

The Henley-on-Todd **Regatta** has to be stopped if it rains and there is water in the river!

Boats without water

During the Henley-on-Todd Regatta, teams race along a dry riverbed in bottomless boats. This festival is held in Alice Springs, Australia.

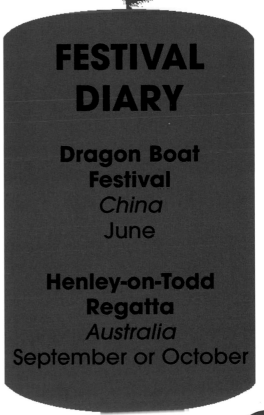

FESTIVAL DIARY

Dragon Boat Festival
China
June

Henley-on-Todd Regatta
Australia
September or October

Special Birthdays

The birth of a religious leader is celebrated with processions and ceremonies.

In some large cities, there are processions and chanting to celebrate Mawlid.

Mawlid

Muslims remember the birth and death of the Prophet Mohammed during the festival of Mawlid. Celebrations are centred around mosques, and there are special feasts and prayers.

Just before the festival, there is a continuous reading of the Sikh's holy book, the Guru Granth Sahib.

Birthday of Guru Nanek Dev

During this Sikh festival, people remember the life of the religion's **founder**, Guru Nanek Dev.

FESTIVAL DIARY

Mawlid
Muslim
April or May

Birthday of Guru Nanek Dev
Sikh
November

I See the Moon

The arrival of a new moon and the full moon are times of celebration.

People make moon cakes for Zhongqui Jie. These have different fillings, such as egg or melon.

Moon poems

Zhongqui Jie celebrates the harvest moon. Lots of people have special parties, and poems and songs are written in praise of the moon.

During the Perahera procession, the Sacred Tooth is carried by an elephant.

Sacred Tooth

Perahera honours a **relic** called Buddha's Sacred Tooth. It is celebrated with a parade that takes place during the full moon in the Buddhist month of Esla.

FESTIVAL DIARY

Zhongqui Jie
China
September

Perahera
Sri Lanka
August

Try This!

Ask an adult to help you with these activities.

Make a very secret Valentine's card

You will need:
- old magazines
- thin coloured card
- glue
- coloured felt-tip pens
- scissors

1 Decide what message you want inside your card. Ask an adult to cut out some letters from a magazine that will spell out this message.

2 Fold the piece of card in half.

3 Use the pens to decorate the front of your card with a large heart.

4 Arrange the letters in order and glue them inside your card (remember not to sign your name).

5 Send your card to your loved one.

Make a tree in blossom for Tet

You will need:
- sheets of pink or yellow tissue paper
- a small branch without any leaves
- green florist's tape
- scissors

1 Place several sheets of tissue paper on top of each other.

2 Ask an adult to cut out lots of small shapes like this through all the layers of paper.

3 Gather the bottom straight edge of each piece of paper in a bunch and spread out the ends in the shape of a blossom.

4 Tape the bottom with florist's tape. Repeat this to make lots of blossoms.

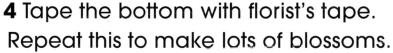

5 Use the florist's tape to attach the blossoms to the branch.

How to Say...

Guru Granth Sahib
say *gu-roo grant sa-hib*

Guru Nanek Dev
say *gu-roo na-nek dev*

Ka'aba
say *ka-ba*

Kwanzaa
say *kwan-zar*

Mawlid
say *maw-lid*

O-Taue
say *o-tow-e*

Perahera
say *pe-ra-he-ra*

Qu'ran
say *cor-ran*

Ramadan
say *ra-ma-dan*

Rosh Hashanah
say *rosh hash-a-na*

Sakura
say *sa-kur-ra*

Songkran
say *song-kran*

Taraweeh
say *ta-ra-wee-eh*

Tet Nguyen-Dan
say *tet n-gooyen-dan*

Zhongqui Jie
say *shong-kee jee*

Glossary

Aborigine
An original inhabitant of Australia.

Blossom
Flowers that grow on trees.

Fasting
A person is fasting when they stop eating.

Founder
A person who starts a group or religion.

Guru Nanek Dev
The Indian religious leader who started the Sikh religion nearly 400 years ago.

Harvest
The gathering or collecting of a crop or animal food source.

Ka'aba
Shrine that holds the most holy Muslim relic – a sacred stone.

Mosque
A Muslim place of worship.

Parade
A march or procession of bands, floats, vehicles and people.

Patron saint
A saint who is chosen by a Christian group to act as a religious guardian.

Prophet
A holy person who is believed to speak the words of God.

Qu'ran
The Muslim holy book.

Ramadan
The Muslim holy month of prayer and fasting.

Regatta
A series of boat races.

Relic
An object that is very old and, in some cases, believed to be very holy.

Shrine
A place that may contain sacred objects and is considered holy.

Synagogue
A Jewish place of worship.

Index